ANDREW GROVE
and the Intel Corporation

Notable Americans

ANDREW GROVE
and the Intel Corporation

Jeremy Byman

MORGAN
REYNOLDS
Incorporated
Greensboro

Andrew Grove and the Intel Corporation

Copyright © 1999 by Jeremy Byman

Library of Congress Cataloging-in-Publication Data
Byman, Jeremy, 1944-
  Andrew Grove and the Intel Corporation / Jeremy Byman.
    p. cm. — (Notable Americans)
  Includes bibliographical references and index.
  Summary: Describes the life of Andrew Grove, the head of the world's leading
producer of microprocessors, which provide the "brains" for the computers in cell
phones, cars, coffeepots, and cameras, as well as personal computers.
  ISBN 1-883846-38-2
    1. Grove, Andrew S. —Juvenile literature. 2. Intel Corporation—History—
Juvenile literature. 3. Semiconductor industry—United States—History—Juvenile
literature.
[1. Grove, Andrew S. 2. Businessmen. 3. Intel Corporation. 4. Semiconductor
industry.]
I. Title II. Series.
HD9696. S42G762 1999
338. 7' 621395' 092—dc21
[B]

                                                                98-49120
                                                                   CIP
                                                                    AC

Printed in the United States of America
First Edition

To Lynn—
for all her encouragement

Contents

Andrew Grove

Chapter One

Andras Grof

In the early 1990s, many predictions were made about how the computer would influence our lives. It was said that people would use hand-held computers as pagers, cell phones, fax machines, personal schedulers and data libraries. These computers would read handwriting and connect to other computers via earth-orbit satellites in a world-wide electronic "net" that would allow people at home and in offices to access words, drawings, photos, and even film clips from huge electronic libraries. People would watch television and computer data simultaneously on flat TV screens. Whole libraries would be put on tiny disks you could carry in your pocket.

While these predictions may have seemed outlandish at the beginning of 1990, before the decade was over, almost all of them came true. It was only a matter of time before a vision that seemed like science fiction would be completely realized.

What all of these technological advances had in common was a little square "chip" made of silicon on which millions of microscopic transistors had been etched by computer-controlled lasers. This tiny self-contained computer the size of a pencil eraser, controlled the operations of computers by making hundreds of millions of calculations a second.

Microprocessors—the "brains" of computers—are everywhere—not just in those computer "boxes" sitting on our desks, such as the one on which this book was written. They're in cell phones, cars, coffeepots, digital cameras, anti-lock brakes, microwave ovens and televisions. They make it possible to communicate by E-mail and surf the Web. They allow movie monsters to go on their exciting rampages.

Microprocessors help to connect the world in a way it has never been connected before. Ideas, pictures, voices, money—anything that can be sent over a phone line or through space—can be transmitted instantly around the world. Trillions of dollars in foreign currencies, stocks and goods of all kinds are traded worldwide each day. Illnesses in distant places can be diagnosed by specialists many time zones away who might never see the patient in person.

At the center of this communications revolution is the leading chip innovator and manufacturer, the Intel Corporation of Santa Clara, California. The man who has led Intel almost from its founding in 1968 and is responsible for his company's commanding lead in the development and sale of the microprocessor has been Andrew Steven Grove.

Andrew Grove, who came to America in 1956 to escape the communist government of his native Hungary, has overseen the world's transformation from an industrial based economy to a technological, post-industrial social structure that has made it increasingly difficult for dictators to oppress their people. Because of computers, video cameras, photocopiers, cell phones and dozens of other inventions, totalitarian governments have discovered that it is no longer a simple matter to restrict the free flow of information. Without controlling what people know, they can't control what people do.

Intel's chips had provided the "brains" for computers long before the giant IBM Corporation unveiled its first personal computer in 1981. But the arrival of a machine that people could use in their home transformed the computer business. Intel, by providing most of the chips for those PCs, led the way.

Today's chips are thousands of times more powerful than those of 1981—and cost only a fraction of the price. This is largely due to the efforts of Grove and the company he ran. Intel has a virtual monopoly in the chip business, manufacturing nearly 90% of the planet's PC microprocessors. As a result, disk-drive manufacturers, software creators and World Wide Web programmers are all dependent on Intel's decisions about how to design and when to release its ever more complex chips.

The man behind this technological revolution was born Andras Grof in Budapest, the capital of Hungary, on September 2, 1936. His father, George, was a dairyman, and his mother, Maria, a bookkeeping clerk.

George Grof was a friendly man who had left school early and taught himself the accounting and business methods he would need to run his small dairy business. The Grof's lived in a tiny, two-room apartment that had been built in the previous century. The family worked hard and encouraged their son to get an education.

When he was four years old, young Andras nearly died from an epidemic of scarlet fever that swept through Budapest. The fever caused a middle-ear infection that perforated his eardrums and left him almost totally deaf. He would later tell an interviewer that he remembered waking up in the hospital and thinking, "I'm dead. I'm in my grave looking up at the sky."

Despite his hearing loss, Andras continued his education. He was clearly an intelligent boy, who was drawn to math and science classes. His future looked bright.

But there was a terrible problem on the horizon. The Grofs were Jewish, and the Nazis, who had come to power in nearby Germany in 1932, had committed themselves to the destruction of all Jews. The Jews in Hungary wondered how long it would be before the Nazis attempted to move into their country.

Then, in September 1939, Nazi Germany invaded Poland. World War II had begun.

Today, Andrew Grove does not talk about his life in Budapest during the war. Although he speaks around the world, he refuses to return to his hometown. There is little known about his war experiences, but what is known helps to explain why the wealthy, successful Andrew Grove of today would rather not reflect on the terrors young Andras Grof faced as a boy.

Early in the war, in 1941, when Hungary was ruled by a government that supported the idea of a Nazi takeover, George

Andrew Grove grew up in Budapest, Hungary.

Grof was drafted into a work brigade and disappeared. Because many other men were disappearing in the same way, Andras and his mother feared the worst.

In March 1944 the Nazis began their occupation of Budapest and began quickly rounding up Jews. They knew that the Russian army was advancing west toward Hungary, and that their time to murder the Jewish population was limited.

When the Nazis arrived, Andras and his mother were already in hiding. Beginning at age eight, Andras spent almost every night eluding the Nazis and their Hungarian allies, who were called the Brownshirts. To help conceal his Jewish identity, his mother gave him a new, Christian name: Andras Malesevics. Mother and son also acquired false papers and lived with a Christian family in order to escape the "pogroms," the government-inspired attacks on the Jews.

"They took us in at a very serious risk to themselves," Andrew remembered years later about the Christian family, in one of his few comments on those years. "I was eight years old, and I knew bad things were happening, but I don't remember the details. My mother took me away. She explained to me what it meant—that I would have a different name, that I cannot make a mistake, that I had to forget my name and I couldn't, if they said 'Write your name,' I couldn't write it down."

Andras and his mother survived the war years by denying their identity and by disappearing into the underground that protected them. By early 1945, the Germans were driven back west, toward their eventual destruction in Germany.

After the fighting ended, it was discovered that George Grof had survived the labor camps on the Eastern front. He had survived, but he had been changed forever. After suffering from typhoid fever and pneumonia, he was no longer the good natured, hard working father Andras had known before the war.

Hungary was ruled by the communists after the war. The communists had their own ideology, or way they thought that the society and the economy should be organized. The first tenet of communism was that private property should be outlawed. They argued that the state should own everything, so there would be no gaps between wealthy and poor. Because private property was outlawed, those who had owned businesses had them taken away. These former successful men and women were also scorned as thieves who had profited from property that should have been shared with everyone.

When Andras was finally able to go back to school, he was mocked by his fellow students for being the son of a business-man. The government considered him and his family to be enemies of the workers. Years later, Andrew remembers the attacks made on him during this period to have been almost as terrible as what he had gone through under the Nazis.

In 1950, when he was a fourteen-year-old high school student, Andras went to work for a youth newspaper. He enjoyed the work, and decided that his future lay in journalism. But the government continued to target his family. A relative was arrested and held without a trial or bail. Andras soon discovered that he wasn't wanted at the newspaper. This was a painful blow to an ambitious and intelligent youngster. He decided that he would go into a profession like science, where he could be judged by what he produced, or the discoveries he made, and not prejudice.

A dedicated student, Andrew soon discovered that he had a talent for chemistry. He could figure out the chemical relationships of a material in his head faster than other people could work them out with a slide rule. He soon began to be noticed as a intelligent science student.

He liked to study sitting in a rowboat in the center of a lake. Friends from those days remember that he was very outgoing and could often be found singing. Most of what he sang was opera. He wanted to combine a career as an opera singer with that of a scientist. He began to take lessons. Once he and some classmates sang a scene from Mozart's famous opera *Don Giovanni* in a Budapest recital.

Although his family still suffered oppression from the Communist Party, and scorn from their neighbors who supported the government, life was good for Andras Grof in the first half of the decade of the 1950s. His family had survived the horrors of World War II, he was successful in school, had friends, and enjoyed the avocation of opera.

The conditions inside Hungary, however, had deteriorated to a breaking point. After the communist seizure of power, many Hungarians shared the Grof's dislike of the new government. Some students began advocating for a more liberal society. Everyone grew weary of the economic system that condemned

In 1956 the citizens of Hungary rebelled against the Soviet domination of their country. These men are celebrating the seizure of a tank.

all but the Communist Party bureaucrats to a life that held no possibility of a better standard of living.

Because of these pressures, some leaders in the Hungarian Communist Party started trying to ease the tight government restrictions on most aspects of the average citizen's life. This led many Hungarians to call for even more freedom. Students began taking to the street, leading marches to demand a fully democratic system.

Although the Hungarian Communist Party held nominal control of the country, the real power in most of the countries of central and eastern Europe that became communist after World War II was the Soviet Union. The Soviets had helped defeat the Nazis by pushing west from its borders. After the fighting stopped, the Soviets established puppet communist governments in most of the nations between the Soviet Union and what was then called West Germany.

As the Soviets watched the events in Hungary, its leaders became more nervous. If Hungary was allowed to stray from the communist system, then they were certain other countries in Eastern Europe would do the same. Soviet Premier Nikita Khrushev decided it was time to end the Hungarian progression toward democracy.

In October of 1956, only a few weeks after Andras performed in *Don Giovanni*, the Red Army of the Soviet Union rolled across the Hungarian border to put down a student uprising. The Soviets had tanks; the students had Molotov cocktails—bottles filled with gasoline and burning pieces of cloth for wicks. It was far from an even fight.

When the Soviet tanks rolled into Budapest, Andras Grof knew it was time to leave his native country. He began to hear rumors of people being rounded up on the street. He had been through this before, when the Germans had controlled Budapest. This time he wasn't going to wait for the Soviets. He headed toward the Hungarian-Austrian border because Austria was not part of the Soviet block of nations.

Many years later, he described his flight to freedom to an interviewer. He and a school friend hopped a train heading west. Twenty miles away from the Austrian border they learned of police checkpoints ahead. They also learned that the Russians were storming through the countryside, arresting everyone they could. They needed to beat the Red Army to the border. They had no one to guide them. They gathered all of their money and bought, from a hunchbacked smuggler, directions to secret routes that the Russians did not know about.

As he neared the border, he could hear the dogs of the border guards barking and snarling. Soldiers fired off flares to light the night sky. Frightened, Andras threw himself face down in the mud. He knew he was near the Austrian border, but he did know how close. Then a voice called out in Hungarian: "Who is there?" He did not know if the smuggler had betrayed him. Should he answer the call, or should he lie silently and hope the searchers didn't find him? Finally, as the steps came closer, Andras asked, "Where are we?" The unseen voice answered, "Austria." Andras Grof had made it to freedom.

Chapter Two

Fairchild Semiconductor

In his race to escape Hungary, Andrew had to leave his parents behind. They had encouraged him to leave, they wanted their bright son to be able to achieve his goals, and knew that he would not have that opportunity in Hungary.

No one had planned on him having to leave so soon. They wanted him to be able to complete his education. But the Soviet tanks had not left time for the Grof family's plans to come to fruition. It would be ten years before he would be able to bring his parents to the United States.

After making it to Austria, Andras joined a large refugee community that lived in Vienna. He immediately began searching for a way to come to America. The International Rescue Committee agreed to sponsor his trip from Vienna to America. Andras Grof, who would soon change his name to the more American-sounding Andrew Grove, was on his way to the United States.

America had always been his goal. Most refugees from communism wanted to come to America, a nearly fabled land of economic prosperity and personal freedom. Few ever had the opportunity.

Andrew made the journey aboard an old ship that had transported American troops during World War II. The ship docked in New York City, where he was processed into the country as a refugee. His refugee status made it easier to go to school and to work. It also would make it easier for him to eventually become a citizen.

Budapest was a large, old city—the capital of Hungary. Andrew had never seen anyplace like New York. He talked years later about the day the International Rescue Committee representative sent him shopping on Fifth Avenue with a blank check to buy the best hearing aid he could find. They had noticed that his hearing was still severely affected by that childhood bout with scarlet fever. (It would take years and over five operations before his hearing was restored to the point he could stop wearing the large, bulky hearing aid.) Andrew has never forgotten this help. Decades later, after he was a wealthy man, he quietly donated money to the agency that helped him come to America and prosper.

Although Andrew did not like New York City, he felt at home in the United States, where people had a better chance of being treated equally than they did back in Europe. In Hungary, "I was always told I was undesirable for one reason or another. I got to the United States, and I expected there would be some of the same because I was an immigrant. And there wasn't."

Andrew was taken in by an aunt and uncle who had come to America two decades earlier. They lived together in a one-bedroom apartment in Brooklyn.

Soon after his arrival, Andrew enrolled at City College of New York. This university system charged no tuition, and had a reputation as a superior school for young people with brains but no money. He quickly became a top student in his major field of study, chemical engineering. Although he still had trouble hearing, he mastered the toughest science classes through hard work.

Andrew earned money during the school year by working as an waiter. After his first year at City College, he worked at a New Hampshire resort as a busboy. While cleaning tables there he met another refugee from Hungary, who was working as a waitress. Eva liked the ambitious young Andrew as much as he liked her, and the young couple were married the following summer, in June of 1958.

Andrew graduated from City College first in his class. He almost earned the highest honor, summa cum laude, but his weakness in the English language got in the way.

"I got a C in Faulkner," he remembered years later. The twentieth century novelist and short story writer William Faulkner is considered to be one of the most difficult of the modern writers to understand. Sometimes his sentences are well over a page in length. This was particularly tough for someone who was in the process of learning English. Grove still remembers the experience with frustration. "My third year speaking English, and I'm reading Faulkner!"

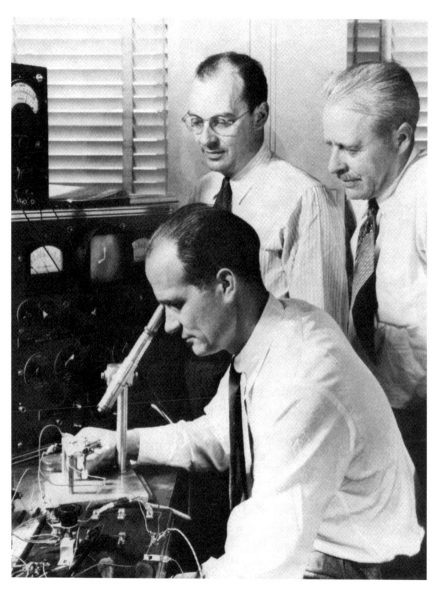

In 1948 William Shockley (seated), John Bardeen (left) and Walter Brattain invented the transistor while working at Bell Labs. The transistor later became the building block for the integrated circuit.

Despite his run-in with modern American literature, Andrew was still a star student at City College. When he graduated in 1960, *The New York Times* published an article about the academic achievements of the recent immigrant.

Andrew was the successful graduate of a respected university, with a degree in a field that almost insured a high demand for his skills. He was also a new husband, and his parents were still living in Hungary. It must have been tempting to find a high paying job and to focus on his immediate responsibilities.

Andrew decided instead to attend graduate school. He wanted to know more about his field, and also realized that more education would eventually benefit his career. Because of his excellent record as an undergraduate, several universities offered him financial assistance. They were eager to attract the brilliant young refugee.

There were several good schools to decide from. Massachusetts Institute of Technology was world famous in his field, and the faculty there was eager for him to attend. But, finally, a desire to escape the cold winters of the northeast swayed his decision of where he would enter graduate school. In 1961, Andrew and Eva moved to California, where he entered the Ph.D. program in chemistry at the University of California at Berkeley. Now he lived near the high technology area of northern California.

At Berkeley, Andrew was again quickly recognized as the star student in the program. He sped through the program with perfect scores, finishing his doctorate degree in three years. Clearly, Andrew Grove was a young man in a hurry.

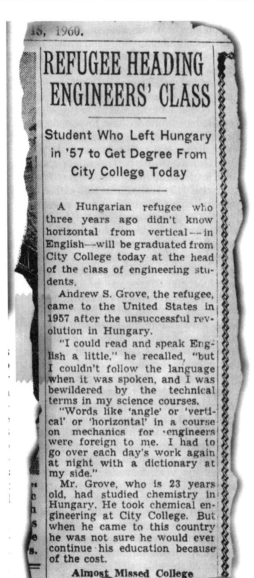

REFUGEE HEADING ENGINEERS' CLASS

Student Who Left Hungary in '57 to Get Degree From City College Today

A Hungarian refugee who three years ago didn't know horizontal from vertical — in English — will be graduated from City College today at the head of the class of engineering students.

Andrew S. Grove, the refugee, came to the United States in 1957 after the unsuccessful revolution in Hungary.

"I could read and speak English a little," he recalled, "but I couldn't follow the language when it was spoken, and I was bewildered by the technical terms in my science courses.

"Words like 'angle' or 'vertical' or 'horizontal' in a course on mechanics for engineers were foreign to me. I had to go over each day's work again at night with a dictionary at my side."

Mr. Grove, who is 23 years old, had studied chemistry in Hungary. He took chemical engineering at City College. But when he came to this country he was not sure he would ever continue his education because of the cost.

Almost Missed College

The New York Times published this article about the achievements of Andrew Grove as a student at the City College of New York.

After graduating from the University of California in 1963, Andrew began entertaining job offers from the most respected high technology companies in the United States. He eventually narrowed his choices down to two.

Bell Laboratories was the most famous organization in the burgeoning field of electronics. It was the home of the transistor, the tiny switch that had replaced the vacuum tube in devices such as radios, televisions and computers. Three scientist from Bell Labs had won the 1948 Nobel Prize in physics for the invention of the transistor.

Any recent graduate would be flattered and well benefited from taking a job at Bell Labs. The salary would be high and, perhaps most importantly, the prestige that could be gained from working at such a highly respected research facility would assure future success.

There was another company that was interested in Andrew Grove, however. Fairchild Semiconductor was a newer and smaller company. It was only six years old in 1963, but in many ways it had carried on the work that was started at Bell. Fairchild had developed a way to put more than one transistor on the same fragment of silicon, a conducting material made from common sand. This was the creation of the "integrated circuit."

Fairchild offered Andrew an opportunity to work on the cutting edge of the new technology. He decided to go to work at Fairchild.

After arriving at his new job in the Research and Development department at Fairchild, Andrew thrived in the atmosphere

The University of California at Berkeley as it looked during the years Andrew was a graduate student in the chemistry department.

of a company that was actually run by a small group of engineers. He hoped that any ideas that came from the his department would not be met with the skeptical questions of a management more concerned about the bottom line than about technological advancement. Later this problem would infiltrate Fairchild, but in the early years, it was an inspiring place to work. Another advantage of working at Fairchild was that he was available to teach classes at nearby Berkeley.

During these years, Andrew and Eva made friends and had an active social life. He also was able to bring his parents to live with him. With his new and expanding career at Fairchild and as a professor, his life in America was full.

But, although he knew many people, no one seemed to know much about him, especially his past. He preferred to think of his life before coming to America as a closed chapter. He listed several Hungarian immigrants among his friends. However, nothing was ever said about his life in the "old country". He never discussed his background with his friends at work. He also did not attend a synagogue, or participate in the local Jewish community. It seemed that, as far as Andrew Grove was concerned, his life started when he sailed into New York harbor.

Occasionally, though, he would make a cryptic comment about his childhood years. He told one friend of how he would be awoken at night by a dream of being chased by a pack of barking dogs. He also admitted that he had hesitated before buying a dog for his two daughters. His mother had recently come to live with him, and he was concerned that the dog would bring back the memories of the German shepherds the Nazis used to herd minorities and political opponents onto the trains that would take them to the death camps.

The normally private Andrew surprised another friend by explaining that the worst part of his childhood experiences was not the misery of the years when he was hiding from the Nazis, but the shame he felt at being told by some of his Hungarian friends after the war that they could not play with because he was a Jew.

During these early years at Fairchild, Andrew was considered a "character" by many who knew him. He sported long sideburns and was fond of wearing colorful shirts. He spoke with a heavy accent and wore a large, awkward hearing aid that wrapped around his head like a set of headphones. His work habits were also exceptional. He put in ten to sixteen hour days during the week, and worked most of the weekends at Fairchild. He also taught at least one class each term at Berkeley, and somehow found time to write a highly respected book about semiconductors.

One thing that his colleagues remember about Grove was his organizational skills. This is the trait that most impressed his bosses at Fairchild, Robert Noyce and Gordon Moore. They soon made him Director of Operations, which gave him control of the day-to-day operations of the entire company.

In 1968, Andrew Grove was thirty-two. His life was an almost miraculous success story: a Jewish boy who had survived the Nazis; an ambitious believer in free enterprise who had escaped the communist government of his native country; the operations manager of one of the most respected high technology companies in the world. It seemed that he lived a charmed life. He could have relaxed and coasted through a successful career, but Andrew Grove was never willing to coast through anything. He was about to be given the chance to take his life into an even more exciting direction.

Chapter Three

The Integrated Circuit

In 1968 Andrew Grove was working in the midst of the revolution brought about by the invention of the semiconductor.

Until 1947, vacuum tubes had been used in the electronic circuits of radios, televisions, and other devices of modern living. Vacuum tubes worked as switches, turning the electric current on or off. Because they functioned by use of a heating element, vacuum tubes needed time to warm up and had to be replaced periodically, much like lightbulbs. They also were large and used vast amounts of electricity. Early computers often filled an entire room that had to be kept very cold because of the heat generated by the vacuum tubes.

When the Bell researchers assembled strips of gold foil, a chip of semiconducting material, and a bent paper clip into the first transistor, the vacuum tubes days were numbered. The tiny transistors also worked as switches, turning on and off electrical impulses. Instead of being heat filled hollow tubes, transistors are solid pieces of semiconducting material (semiconducting material such as silicon can both conduct current, like copper, or insulate the current, like rubber.) And, unlike vacuums, transistors do not generate excess heat. Early in the 1950s devices were changed to accommodate the new discovery. Small, cheap pocket "transistor radios" soon became the rage among teenagers. The fuller possibilities of the semiconductor were slower to be realized, however.

In 1957, Robert Noyce and Gordon Moore hoped that Fairchild Semiconductor would find a way to use the new transistor technology to advance the development of the digital computer. Previously, most attempts to speed up computers failed because they still used vacuum tubes as giant on-off switches to hold and release electrical charges. These on-off signals were converted into ones and zeroes and then into real numbers. Not only were the tubes expensive to operate and very hot, they were also slow to process the information. There was also little storage capacity and very little operating memory. There needed to be a way to make computers smaller, faster, and easier to use.

Fairchild wanted to achieve this goal by using the transistor. The on-off signals of the transistor switch could be converted into ones and zeroes ("binary numbers"). The problem was to find a pure chemical surface that would move electrons efficiently. The solution turned out to be silicon, a naturally occurring element found in common sand. Its discovery as the right substance to use in transistors would be immortalized in the nickname of the area south of San Francisco where many computer companies are located: Silicon Valley.

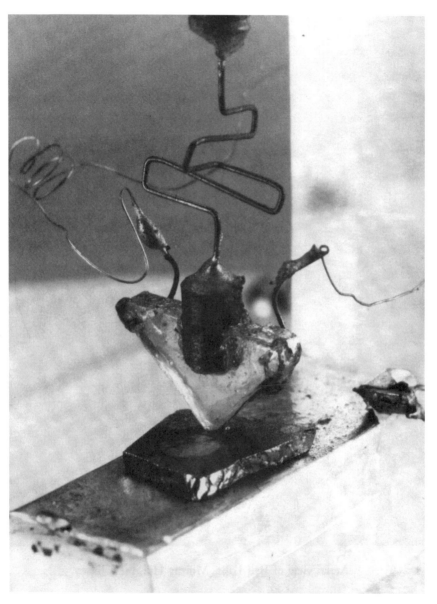

A replica of the first transistor. It could amplify a signal one hundred times.

The great virtue of silicon is that it efficiently conducts electrical charges while drawing off excess heat. And because it was refined from sand, the supply would always be abundant.

One transistor, however, did not provide enough memory. There was still the task of combining several into electrical circuits. Bob Noyce had co-created a method of putting more than one transistor on a single piece of silicon, creating the "integrated circuit" in 1959. This invention opened the way for the development of more powerful computers.

The process of creating an integrated circuit had to be tightly controlled. Crystalline silicon made from sand was molded into the shape of a long sausage about two inches in diameter, and then sliced into wafers a fraction of an inch thick. Dozens of identical miniature circuits were mounted on the wafers and aligned in rows and columns. Next, the wafers had grooves scored into them with a diamond-cutter. Finally, the chips would be separated and wired individually into black ceramic packages. The circuits built this way were connected, or "integrated circuits."

After the invention of the integrated circuit, the challenge was to find a way to mass produce them that would guarantee a large supply. This was the challenge that faced Fairchild, or any other company that moved into the business, in 1968.

Gordon Moore had a perception about the future of the integrated memory chip in 1965. He drew a graph showing that the power of microchips would double every eighteen months, even as the cost fell by half. So far, this prediction has been

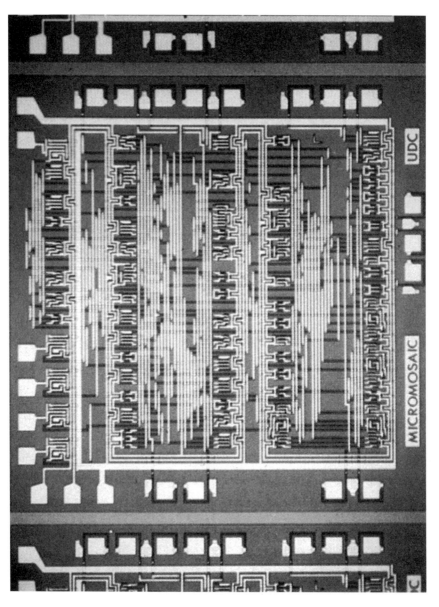

A chip made by Fairchild in 1967. The transistors are the dark, horizontal lines.

proven to be true, and has become known as Moore's Law.

What Moore's Law also did was guide chip manufacturers in anticipating demand for its chips. If the price of a semiconductor was cut in half every eighteen months, then you could predict when the newer developments would be cheap enough to gain widespread use. For example, it was easy to know when it would be cost effective to put a tiny microprocessor in a wristwatch, exercise equipment, or a microwave.

Ironically, Moore did not at first realize that his rule would affect the business of making chips for computers more than any other industry. This was a failure of imagination on his part. He did not envision the day of the desktop, much less the laptop, computer. To Moore, computers would only be of use to corporations and other large organizations.

Many years later, in 1987, it was much more obvious what Gordon Moore, Intel, and other technology companies were bringing about. An IBM personal computer in 1987 had twice the power, at 1/34th the price, of an IBM mainframe computer sold in 1975. Looking back on his now famous law, Moore explained his failure to see the immense dimensions of the coming computer revolution: "If the same kind of progress had been made in the auto industry over the past seven years," he said, "you'd go a million miles per hour and get half-a-million miles to a gallon of gas. It would be cheaper to throw your Rolls away than park it downtown in the evening. I thought that was a neat analogy until someone pointed out that the Rolls would be only six inches long and two inches wide."

But in the mid-1960s there was the problem of producing enough chips to put Moore's Law into operation. Fairchild was still an innovative company that presented challenging engineering problems. Andrew Grove thrived in the high pressure environment. On his very first day, he was asked to study a critical problem that had arisen with the new integrated circuits. The base of the circuit, metal-oxide-on-silicon, or MOS, was highly unstable. The failure rate of the silicon wafers was as high as 90% because of this instability. This problem needed to be fixed in order to make production of the integrated circuit possible at a success level that would guarantee profits.

After several months work, Andrew and his colleagues discovered that the problem came in the "curing" stage of production, when the sodium was introduced. It was a critically important finding. It made it possible for semiconductors and integrated circuits to begin their rapid evolution into the microchips we know today.

Chapter Four

The 1103

By 1968, Bob Noyce and Gordon Moore, the top scientists at Fairchild Semiconductor, had grown frustrated. Because of the way the company had been founded, all the critical decisions were made at the corporate headquarters in New York. After their early success in creating new products, it became clear that the company's leadership was more concerned with making immediate profits than investing in cutting edge technology for the future. The two men knew that a company that rested on its laurels was not going to survive long in the fast paced, high technology industry.

Many of Fairchild's top researchers had already left when Noyce and Moore decided to start their own company. They went to a local venture capitalist, a man who helped start-up companies find money. Because of their respected reputations in the electronics field, Noyce and Moore were able to raise the money they needed to start their own semiconductor company in a matter of days. The two men originally thought of calling their company Integrated Electronics because they were going to be building integrated circuits. After deciding the name was too "old fashioned" they shortened it to the Intel Corporation.

As soon as word got out that Noyce and Moore were forming a new company, they were swamped with resumes and phone calls from engineers who wanted to come to work at Intel. It became apparent that the new company could have its pick of the brightest engineers.

Andrew Grove was one person Noyce and Moore wanted to join Intel. They had been impressed with his abilities at Fairchild, especially his talents at organization. These skills would complement Noyce and Moore, both of whom had spent most of their careers in research and development. One of their first decisions was to offer Grove the job of Director of Operations. Andrew accepted immediately. It would be another six years, however, before he was acknowledged as the third member of the founding group.

The new company's first location was an old Union Carbide plant, located fifty miles south of San Francisco. Intel's initial goal was to make memory devices for the mainframe computers that corporations used to run accounting programs and store payroll and medical records. Those computers needed to be able to retrieve data files quickly in order to more fully benefit from the new technology. The calculations were being done by Noyce's integrated circuits at much faster operating speeds than the vacuum tube technology had been able to deliver. But the data had to be placed into storage, or "memory" several times during an operation.

These memory devices were still the old-fashioned magnetic core technology. Magnetic core technology was a generation behind the integrated circuit. Computers could now do calculations in a fraction of a second, but when it had to retrieve and store the information, it had to stop and wait for the magnetic core to do its work.

Intel wanted to create faster memory devices with more storage capacity so that computers would be more compact and speedier. There were several competing ideas of how best to achieve this goal. Intel decided to put most of their energy behind what was called the "silicon gate" technology, which had been researched at Fairchild. It was Fairchild's inability to develop this technology, a failure Noyce and Moore attributed more to office politics than to the technological difficulties, that had prompted them to form Intel.

The "silicon gate" concept, a variation on the integrated circuit, used metal oxide and silicon transistor chips encased in air-tight ceramic. The development of the so-called MOS chip was a difficult project. Many of the problems occurred during the production, when the chip was baked to form a glass enclosure to hold it together. This airtight sealed chamber could then be connected to a circuit board by tiny wire pins.

Before the MOS chip could be released, it was necessary to solve these problems so the chips could be produced in adequate amounts. The chips were highly fragile, and, early in its development, the vast majority were useless when they rolled off the

The founders of Fairchild Semiconductor. Gordon Moore is on the far left. Robert Noyce is the fourth from left.

assembly line. The chips were cracking as they were heated and cooled. Grove even grew impatient with the high failure rate and began advocating abandonment of the MOS technology. He suggested they pursue other means of making memory chips. Gordon Moore, however, calmly suggested that impurities be added to the oxide portion of the chip that would reduce the element's melting-point. This would allow the chips to be "cooked" at a lower heat and reduce chances of cracking. Moore's suggestion solved the cracking problem. This episode taught Andrew quite a bit about maintaining his composure and being patient in the face of technological difficulties.

The cracking during production was an example of the often maddening problems that popped up during the two years it took to develop the MOS chip. But the engineers at Intel, many of whom were young and willing to work eighteen-hour days, persisted.

In 1970, Intel finally began marketing its new semiconductor memory chip. The new design was given the number 1101, which began a twenty-year tradition of Intel numbering its products instead of naming them. (This practice was eventually discontinued because of difficulties in earning patent protection for inventions that had not been named.) This new integrated-circuit memory chip was labeled "dynamic random access memory," or DRAM, to distinguish it from the old style magnetic core memory. For a while, Intel was only supplier of semi-conductor memory. Eventually, they began "outsourcing" some of the chip production because the demand was simply too high for them to meet in their manufacturing facilities.

The Moore's Law prediction of falling costs, rising performance and diminishing size began to be proved to be true. The price of semi-conductor memory fell so far, so fast, over the next two decades that the tiny chips would start showing up in all kinds of electronic devices, and created billions of dollars in profits to Intel.

In 1970, however, there was still many improvements to be made. The 1101 was soon upgraded to 1103, but it was still far from perfect. It was difficult for the computer manufacturers of that era, companies like Honeywell and IBM, to use. It required extra circuits and power supplies. These large customers were soon pressuring Intel to correct the flaws in the 1103. But it was still vastly superior to the old magnetic core memories in both speed and capacity. After two years, Intel was making a steady profit. There would be more innovations, and profits, in the future.

Chapter Five

The Microprocessor

Despite its flaws, the 1103 memory chip made Intel a highly successful company. In only two years, the upstart company had vaulted in front of its competition. The depressed engineers who had stayed behind at Fairchild had to watch the new company take ideas that had first been developed in their laboratory and turn them into successful products. Several decided it was time to call Andrew Grove and ask him for a job. Intel was now the place for the most talented engineers to work.

The development of the 1103 was impressive. But Intel's next technological advancement would be unprecedented. And it would come about almost accidentally. The development of the first microprocessor began as a quick and dirty way to get around a seemingly insurmountable problem.

In the early years there was a standard rule about the designing of new chips: "One man, one chip, one year." One man (there were very few women chip designers) would spend one year to develop a chip. This changed during an Intel project began in 1970, when an engineer designed four working chips in three months—and invented the first microprocessor.

Intel's development of one of the most important technological advancements in the twentieth century began when a Japanese calculator company called Busicom contracted with Intel to create a set of eight logic chips. Logic chips were designed to carry out specific tasks. In this case, the chips were needed to perform the math functions the company wanted to offer in its calculators.

Intel took the contract—and then realized they would not be able to produce the chips. There simply was not enough manpower in the company. They had over-promised on the delivery date. The Japanese company would not get its chips and would probably have grounds to sue Intel for damages. It was a difficult situation, and the pressure inside the company was intense.

Finally, one engineer had an idea. Why not make the calculator a small computer?

The difference between a calculator and a computer in 1970 was that a calculator could only do one function to completion before moving on to another. A computer could stop what it was doing, do something else, then return to the original task. This function was called sub-routine capability. Computers were able to do this because of their processor units and the software that told the processor what to do. What the engineer suggested was to combine all the processes needed to operate the calculator into a set of simple sub-routines to be stored on a tiny processor made of four chips. The calculator would be turned into a limited computer.

The immediate appeal of this idea was that it would allow

Intel to meet its deadline. All they would need to do was develop four chips, although they would be more sophisticated. After convincing Busicom to take a risk with the new idea, Intel began work on the new processor.

The original design for the processor remained the same throughout the project. The four-chip set consisted of a central processing unit (CPU), a memory chip for storage of active data, a read-only memory chip (ROM) to store the software program written to control the calculator's functions, and a fourth chip to modulate input and output of data (I/O).

Because Intel designed the microprocessor under contract for another the company, the Japanese firm had full rights to the processor upon completion. But then Busicom complained that they needed to cut the price on their calculator in order to be able to compete in the market. They wanted Intel to lower the price on the chips from what was established on the original contract.

Grove, Noyce and Moore agreed to discount $60,000 off on one condition—Intel would retain full rights on the new processor. Busicom agreed to the change, and Intel retained the rights to the product that has made it the most successful chip maker in the world.

The new microprocessor was dubbed the 4004. It's power roughly matched that of the ENIAC, the first vacuum tube computer built in 1946. But the ENIAC filled a large room and had eighteen thousand vacuum tubes, while the 4004 was smaller than a matchbox.

Most computer manufacturers ignored the 4004. Computer

The first microprocessor had approximately the same power as the ENIAC, the first computer built during World War II.

power had grown a thousandfold since 1946. The 4004 could only process four bits of information at a time, much less than the bestselling mainframe computers. It just did not occur to the leaders of IBM, Honeywell, or Digital Electronics that such a tiny device could ever have enough power to drive a marketable computer.

The leading computer manufacturers had missed the point, of course. They were fooled by the tiny size of the microprocessor, and didn't understand that it was a miniature general-purpose computer that could be made more and more powerful. One executive even said that his customers would not buy a computer that could be lost through a crack in the floor.

Computer makers were not the only ones who failed to see the future. No one at Intel, including the very top managers, envisioned a society where individuals would want to own their own computers. Why would the average family ever need a computer? They had no payroll to figure, or products to manufacture, or huge databases that needed to be managed. It simply never occurred to them that there was a market for the desktop computer.

Intel decided that the new microprocessor could be used best in small business machines like cash registers and coin change machines, or in more domestic products like microwave ovens. Any small electronic machine that needed to be programmable to enhance its features could benefit from the 4004.

Even within this narrow vision, there were some problems marketing the 4004. The biggest drawback was that it was

The 4004 microprocessor was built almost by accident.

difficult to program. There were no compilers—programs that organize another program to work on a specific machine. This meant that the most fundamental functions had to be written in assembly-language instructions for the chip, telling it step by step to input this data, store it in that register, add it to the contents of the other register, output the result, and so on. After the program was assembled, then it had to be turned into workable code. It was tedious, frustrating work. There were thousands of lines and one mistake could render the entire processor inoperable.

In 1972 Intel released an updated microprocessor called the 8008. This new chip was more powerful and easier to program than the 4004, and sales to small appliance manufacturers and other similar companies increased.

Two customers for the 8008 were teenagers from Seattle, Washington: Paul Allen and Bill Gates. The two high school students planned to write programs in the BASIC computer language and to have the microprocessor support it. But the 8008 was not up to the job. When this scheme failed, the two high schoolers launched a small company to count cars that passed on streets for municipal governments. The machine they built to do their work used the 8008. This was the first, but certainly not the last, time Intel came in contact with the future founders of Microsoft Corporation.

While the 4004 processed only four bits of information at a time, the 8008 could process eight bits—a doubling of computer power. Moore's Law was again proven to be true.

As exciting as these new chips were, it was not innovation alone that gave Intel its commanding position in the chip industry. It was also better than other companies at distributing its products, offering a wide range of products, and providing service and programs that would help customers put their chips to best use.

When Intel created a new type of memory chip, it threw its marketing apparatus into full gear. The new product was called the "erasable, programmable, read-only memory" chip, or EPROM. The EPROM was an advance on the simple memory chip. Before, Read Only Memory (ROM) chips were designed

Two students from Seattle, Bill Gates (standing) and his friend Paul Allen, tried to use the 8008 processor in a small, home-build computer.

with the necessary data burned into them. This meant that the necessary circuits were designed, then etched into the silicon wafers during the fabrication process. This was a painstaking process that often resulted in useless chips.

With EPROM new data could be written into a chip in seconds and, if a mistake was made, it could be "erased" by use of an ultraviolet light and new information could be added. This product would make designing computers much easier, and demand would increase if engineers knew of its potential.

Intel decided to roll out the new product with a bang. At the 1971 International Solid State Circuits Conference, Intel presented a movie to the gathering of engineers, circuit designers, and other research and development professionals. The film showed a series of bits being erased, one by one, until it revealed the Intel logo. This simple, dramatic demonstration of how easy the new EPROM was to use caused the audience to burst out in spontaneous applause. The product looked to be a smashing success.

Then, as manufacturing started up, almost all the chips had to be thrown away. They did not work. After investigation showed that a simple adjustment in the voltage used to write data into the chip solved the problem, production began again.

However, in the process of fixing the production problem, it was discovered that EPROM worked well with the new 8008 microprocessor. Because any company that used the microprocessor would also need to store the program that commanded the processor, it made sense to also buy the new erasable memory. Although EPROM was more expensive, it was so much easier to work with customers that were willing to pay the extra cost. The fact the solution to these problems had happened almost by accident, meant that it was less likely to be discovered by Intel's competition.

Andrew Grove was always in the middle of solving these problems. His influence spread far beyond the normal duties of Director of Operations. It soon became clear to new hires that he was the one person in charge. He still looked a bit like a "hippie" in the early 1970s. He wore gold chains, muttonchop whiskers and thick glasses. He still wore the huge hearing aid that looked like headphones on top of his wild, bushy hair.

Grove's hard-driving management style sometimes made him hurtful and insensitive. But he was also a brilliant problem solver. His attention to detail drove some lesser disciplined workers to distraction. But his absolute determination to not let even the most difficult problems stop development influenced the other workers. He drove himself as hard as he drove everyone else.

The pressure was enormous. Noyce and Moore expected Andrew to produce chips of acceptable quality quickly and cheaply. This led to occasional explosions at production and sales meetings. The sales manager, who had invented the marketing slogan "Intel Delivers," would complain that customers weren't getting the promised chips. Why hadn't Andrew delivered all that he said he would deliver? Grove would yell back with his thick Hungarian accent and the room would fill with charges and counter-charges.

Sometimes, when he was about to be told something he didn't want to hear, Andrew's hearing aid would suddenly "fail" and he would began bellowing "Huh? Huh?" Another favorite Andrew Grove trick was to use his hearing aid to make a more demonstrative point. When a speaker at a meeting was running over the allotted time, or straying from the point, he would take the hearing aid off his head and thump it down on the table. This was his way of saying that he was finished listening. There might be arguments, but it was clear to everyone that Andrew was in charge.

By the mid-1970s, Intel was known around the world for having invented the microprocessor, the DRAM computing memory chip and the EPROM storage memory chip. It employed over 3,000 people at three plants in the United States, and had two overseas plants to handle the final packaging of chips. In seven years it had moved into a commanding position in the chip design and manufacturing industry. But even Andrew Grove and the other minds behind Intel had no idea of the changes that were soon to sweep their industry and, eventually, the entire world.

Chapter Six

McIntel

Intel continued to improve the microprocessor. In 1974, computing power doubled again with the introduction of the 8080. The new processor was an eight-bit processor with 8,000 transistors, and was powerful enough to be used in data-processing applications.

Andrew Grove was now being publicly recognized as one of the three founders of Intel. His title was executive vice-president, and he was the company's operations manager in name as well as in fact. Gordon Moore still made the overall decisions about the company's strategies and goals, and Robert Noyce was traveling around the world representing the company in meetings with governments and industry.

Andrew's job had gotten more difficult over the years. The competition to make chips smaller, faster and cheaper was intense, and the number of things that could go wrong in the making of ever more powerful chips seemed to multiply. Sometimes, of a hundred chips on a wafer of silicon, only five were usable. In any other business, such yields would been disastrous—the plant manager would have been fired. But it was different with computer chips. There were substantial start-up cost with each chip. But once the engineering was completed, it was possible to make a profit, even with so much waste, because the raw materials were so cheap. For a few cents worth of silicon and other materials, a chip that could be sold for hundreds of dollars could be produced.

Still, in Andrew's view, there was no reason to pass up chances to improve profitability in production. He liked changes that increased efficiency. He tried anything to decrease costs because this allowed prices to be cut enough to maintain a competitive edge in the market. He experimented with doubling the number of usable chips per wafer, increasing the size of the wafers, and decreasing the circuit size. When one of these experiments worked he kept it. If it failed, something else was tried.

In the 1960s and early 1970s, it was still possible to make changes like these by assigning an individual engineer to the design problem—"one man, one chip, one year." But now the designs were so complicated that huge teams, sometimes more a hundred people, were needed. First, a circuit designer drew a design. This could take months, working long hours with an assistant who cut the circuit designs into a giant sheet of rubylith. After repeated checking of the design, over a period of weeks, the first prototypes could be fabricated.

The constant pressure to increase efficiency made Intel's fabrication plants stressful places to work. Procedures were always changing. There would be a new piece of equipment to learn how to operate, new processes to master. Workers had to wear protective suits with white, surgical style booties and a cap, called a "snood," over their hair. Much of the work entailed attaching tiny wires that could not be misplaced by even the smallest degree. A mistake of 1/32 of an inch in placing a wire could render a chip inoperable.

Andrew wanted to see a consistency in the product from different plants similar to the consistency of fast food hamburgers. This earned his company the nickname "McIntel." He also opposed any unionization, which might raise costs and reduce the efficiency of his operation.

It was in this setting of rapid change and rigorous competition that Andrew began to develop his theories of management, which reflected his own strong personality. He advocated what he called "constructive confrontation"—intense discussions about the challenges they faced. The trick was to do this without actually getting people angry at each other.

Andrew also set the daily goals he expected of his managers. He demanded them to come up with detailed dollar figures for their costs and expenses, and to explain why any changes were necessary. He also expected everyone, including himself, to come up with regular lists of "key results" that they were promising to achieve.

One of Grove's favorite type of meetings were called "one-on-ones." During these sessions an employee's performance was evaluated and pay raises were determined. There were also monthly meetings in which department heads were forced to make presentations to and to take ideas from employees who did not work in their area. Occasionally, top managers went on retreats to consider the bigger, strategic questions about the company's future, such as what type of new products should be designed, what new markets could they try to open, or where to place new plants.

Andrew liked to chat with people in their offices, as part of on-going walking tours he took at fabrication plants. During these walking tours he covered every inch of the building, checking on everything from the janitor's cubbyhole to the cleanliness of the boardroom. Grove had an intense fixation on tidiness. One employee remembered that: "You wouldn't get an immediate pay cut if there were too many papers in your in-box or a pile of books on the floor. But you'd get asked pointed questions—about whether you had just come back from a business trip that accounted for the backlog of unanswered mail, or whether you were waiting for a new bookcase to arrive— which made it clear that the company viewed untidiness as incompatible with doing your job properly."

Grove also began requiring exit interviews to be conducted when employees left the company. Andrew thought something useful could be learned from someone who was leaving. If the employee was unhappy, it may be possible to avoid making other employees dissatisfied. It was critical that Intel hold on to its best workers.

All of these measures were intended to be businesslike and

Andrew Grove, Bob Noyce, and Gordon Moore in 1975.

impersonal. But sometimes Andrew seemed to turn "constructive" into "aggressive." Maybe it was because of his tough childhood, but Andrew Grove never backed down from a fight. Some thought he took pleasure in shouting at people. One senior manager happened to be in his office when Grove took a call from a subordinate who was asking for authority to spend money on something. Grove refused the request. Then he scolded the man angrily. When he hung up the phone, he turned calmly to the colleague who had witnessed the telephone conversation and said, "That got his attention, I think."

Intel grew so quickly, and rate of change so rapid, that even those who did not work in the fabrication plants had to contend with turmoil. One problem was that there was always a demand for new offices. As soon as someone was settled into a new space, workmen showed up to take down a wall, or to decrease the office size, to accommodate new hires. Sometimes a wall would be built and taken down within a month. It became difficult to get any work done because of the noise, dust, and inconvenience.

Andrew finally hit upon a solution to this problem. He decided to abolish offices altogether. Offices were replaced with cubicles—a small working area with a desk, chair, bookshelf and telephone, surrounded by a shoulder-high padded dividers. The walls on these spaces could be moved in a moment. The other hope was that the new workspace would break down many of the communication barriers that plagued growing businesses. Some of the employees hated the new design. They preferred

An early Intel advertisement for the microprocessor.

the old style offices with doors that could be shut. Other employees, however, liked the open design and not having to deal with the constant construction. Grove made certain that everyone, including himself, had a cubicle. This way there would not be any claims of privilege. Eventually, this cubicle idea spread through much of America's business.

As Intel grew, it became necessary to develop security measures to guard its secrets. More and more companies were suing each other over copyright infringements. Sometimes companies would register a patent, then lease the right to reproduce it to other companies. Sometimes an engineer would leave one company for another and take the knowledge he or she had learned at Intel to the new company. Grove began pressuring Intel managers to sign contracts that prevented them from moving quickly to competitors, or that prohibited other companies to profit from their chip designs. The effort to save trade secrets began taking up more and more of Grove's time. As the years progressed, Intel would become the chip manufacturer most willing to use the courts to protect itself, and to break down the secrecy of its competitors.

In 1976 threats to the company's profitability emerged from an unexpected source. Several Japanese companies had begun producing computer chips. Initially, they found it hard to establish a market among the American appliance and computer makers. Their solution was to begin "dumping" chips—selling them below cost—onto the market. The strategy was to run the other companies out of business. Then, the dumpers would be able to raise their prices and profit from the lack of competition.

This problem with Japanese competition grew worse over the next few years. Japanese companies were not only making copied chips more cheaply, but by 1979 they were starting to bring out advanced memory chips cheaper and faster than Americans could. Clearly, an American company was going to have to find a new way to survive. It was not going to be possible to beat the Japanese in the low-cost memory chip market.

Andrew Grove and the rest of the Intel management continued to be slow to realize the potential of the personal computer. When a few of its engineers suggested putting the new 8080 processor in a box with a keyboard and a monitor and marketing it as a microcomputer, Gordon Moore wasn't interested. He saw the software problem as being insurmountable. You would have to make the computer easy enough for the average user, he said. This would demand hundreds of different programs to type letters, update addresses, and keep track of household spending, and so on. No household could afford, or would want, the enormously expensive programs that the industry used. In other words: Why did anyone but the largest corporations and government entities need the power of a computer? He could not envision such a market.

One of the reasons Intel made this mistake was that their current customers were not the so-called "end-users." They were companies that put the chips and processors into their products, then sold the appliances, computers, stop lights, and other items to those who actually put it to work. Being one layer away from the chips actual user meant that Grove and others simply could not see the vast potential of the average buyer, and missed a chance to become the world's first personal computer manufacturer.

Even as Moore was listing his objections, the microcomputer market was starting to grow—and it was made possible, at least partly, by Intel. A small company in New Mexico began advertising a personal computer kit that could be built on any kitchen top. Altair's kit used an Intel 8080 as its processor and the young computer enthusiasts from Seattle, Bill Gates and Paul Allen, began writing computer languages for the new Altair 8800.

Nearby in northern California, Steve Jobs and Steve Wozniak designed and began marketing a computer under the name of Apple. For a while, from the late 1970s through the first half of the 1980s, Apple would set the standard as the personal computer maker of choice. Apple had received much needed funding from a former Intel employee who had invested his Intel stock earnings. Apple's new computer was built around a microprocessor sold by Motorola, one of Intel's biggest competitors.

But, even after these dramatic developments, and the creation of software written for small computers, Intel still ignored this new market. But this would have to change if the company that had only a decade before been on the cutting edge of computer technology wanted to survive in the accelerating computer industry.

Chapter Seven

Enter Big Blue

Andrew Grove was the one person at Intel who refused to let the company rest on its laurels. Although his attention had not focused on the microcomputer, he seemed to sense the intense competition and opportunities that waited just over the horizon. While the chip designs became even more revolutionary, he introduced ever more elaborate ways to manage the company's growth. He created a new system called "Management By Objectives" that required every aspect of production to be measured. Production managers counted the number of chips produced, the bookkeeping department counted the number of checks written, even the janitors counted the number of square feet of floor space cleaned. To some it seemed excessive, but Grove was always looking ahead.

In 1979, Andrew Grove became president and COO (chief operating officer) of Intel. Gordon Moore became chairman and CEO (chief executive officer,) and Bob Noyce was shifted to vice-chairman—he was no longer involved with the company on a daily basis. But once again, the change in titles didn't actually mean a change in what Andrew was doing, or what he expected from himself and other people.

Andrew participated in all aspects of the company's operation. He even made sales calls. Unlike other salesmen, he was all business when he called on a customer. He didn't entertain at the company's expense, or spend time telling jokes, before getting to the point. He was not afraid to call chip designers in the middle of the night with a question if he was going to be in a meeting with an important customer the next morning. If the customer balked at the terms of the sale, Grove thanked him for his time and left quickly.

But not even Grove's efforts as a salesman, or his management innovations, could help when business slumped in the late 1970s. Intel had invented the first dynamic random access memory chip, the first erasable memory chip, and the first microprocessor. But, despite its success in design and production, they still had to compete with competitors who had their own innovations to offer. As the market shrank, partly due to a weak economy and partly to more intense competition, the company that had blazed the trail in chip and processor design clearly needed to find new ways to grow.

Intel would not have survived if it had continued to ignore the microcomputer market. Fortunately, persistence, a little luck—and some tough business practices—intervened to save them from their own lack of foresight.

In 1978, Intel released two nearly-identical chips. Despite an inelegant design, both the 8086 and the 8088 offered major improvements in chip processing power. Each had 30,000 transistors, more than ten times the number in the 4004. For the first time, an Intel chip used a sixteen-bit word length, allowing it to receive 64,000 instructions a second. This meant that more demanding programming languages could be used to write better software. The new processors were the first to include microcode—miniature programs that could simplify complex instruction sets.

These new features gave the chips more flexibility and speed, which allowed computer makers to build systems with up to one million bytes (a megabyte) of memory. But the new chips biggest selling point with both computer makers and users was that they provided for "backward-compatibility." Old programs could be used with the new chip, even while software companies dreamed up more programs that could take full advantage of the chip's more powerful features.

This was a new concept in microprocessor design and was a stroke of genius from a marketing point of view. Backward-compatibility meant that once a company began designing its computer and programmers began writing code around an Intel processor, it would have a strong incentive to continue doing so with each new generation of chip. If old software could run on the new chip, it was easier for a computer company to decide to use the latest design. Therefore, nothing was rendered obsolete or incompatible. Why ever change processors and have to totally redesign software every two years? Grove had even given the chips numbers that suggested they were linked in a "family" of compatible products.

When the sales department reported back to Grove that customers were saying that Motorola's processors were cheaper, faster and easier to use, he created an elaborate public relations effort called Operation Crush. The goal was to persuade the industry that Intel's chips were the best. Intel stressed its industry leadership, its interrelated family of products, and its excellent sales force and customer service. Also important was the fact that the 8086 and 8088 were part of an electronic package that worked better than anyone else's because it had a math coprocessor built into the design that sped up computation. He also released a catalogue advertising chips that had not yet been designed, much less manufactured.

The plan was to create such a stir in the marketplace that Intel would set the terms of the debate. Hopefully, the competition would shift focus and begin to plan their future around Intel's plans. Once this happened, Grove knew it was inevitable that his company would emerge the winner.

Motorola took the bait and began replying to Intel's advertising claims, instead of pushing its own products. By the end of 1980, it was clear that Intel had won the battle. They were now the dominant maker of microprocessors in the world.

The shift of emphasis from selling memory chips to selling microprocessors could not have happened at a better time. Grove's Operation Crush placed Intel in the perfect position to

A chip on an electronic tester. The probes put each integrated circuit through a battery of tests.

take advantage of the biggest leap forward to have ever occurred in the small computer market.

Over the years, one computer company Intel had never had good relations with was IBM, the giant builder of mainframes. Early in its history, Intel had angered IBM by making replacement and add-on parts for their computers—and by selling them for half as much as "Big Blue" charged. Over the years, however, IBM had relaxed it attitude toward the upstart chipmaker slightly, and had even contracted for some of Intel's memory chips to be used in its printers and other peripheral products. But the atmosphere between the two companies was still charged with tension and suspicion.

Early in 1980, rumors began sweeping the computer industry that IBM was going to begin building and selling a microcomputer. This so-called Personal Computer, or PC, would be marketed primarily to small and medium size businesses that had never had the benefit of computer power before. Finally, a large company was seeing a viable future market for desktop computers. Whereas Gordon Moore and others at Intel had resisted building a small computer because they saw no way individuals would use it, IBM concluded that the real market for PCs was small businesses. This decision changed the computer world forever.

IBM, determined to keep its plans top secret, assigned two groups the task of designing the new machine. One group in Texas contracted with Motorola to build the PC around the same processor used in the Apple II. Another group, located in

Florida, decided to work with Intel's 8088.

Because IBM was determined to keep its plans secret, the Intel salesmen and engineers who called on the Florida site were never told why IBM was interested in purchasing thousands of 8088 chips.

Ironically, IBM sometimes found it necessary to have Intel consult with them on the design of the PC. When the Intel field engineers called on the IBM design facility in Florida they found they had to do their consulting work in a strange environment. One Intel employee remembered the meetings he had with the IBM engineers was more than tense. "They'd have their technical people on one side of a black curtain and ours on the other," he said later. "We'd ask questions; they'd tell us what was happening and we'd try to solve the problem literally in the dark. If we were lucky, they'd let us reach a hand through the curtain and grope around a bit to try to figure out what the problem was."

Every effort was made to secure the PC project. But IBM could not keep its secret forever. It soon became clear that they had big plans—and that their plans included Intel. During the negotiations, the computer manufacturer demanded guarantees that Intel could meet the demand for chips. They even insisted that Intel arrange for "second sourcing," which meant that Intel had to contract with another chip manufacturer to provide production support to guarantee IBM an ample supply of the processors. Intel contracted with a competing California company in order to please IBM.

Eventually, Intel learned that Motorola had not been able to produce the chips in time to meet IBM's demand. Intel would be the supplier of the microprocessors for the IBM PC, the first desktop computer to be marketed by a major corporation. By late 1981, the television airwaves were filled with commercials of a Charlie Chaplin look-a-like convincing millions of American small businesses, and some homes, that they needed to buy a computer built by IBM with an Intel processor inside.

The arrangement with IBM was going to lift Intel into a much higher level of profitability and influence. But all of its moves in this new microcomputer field were not as wise, or as profitable. When the head of a software company located in Redmond, Washington flew down to Intel with his company's new operating system, called MSDOS, the Intel engineers were less than impressed. Bill Gates wanted Intel to endorse his product, and to license it to be used with the 8086 and 8088 microprocessor. A financial arrangement between Intel and Microsoft would have joined the two companies with IBM, who had already agreed to use MSDOS in its new PCs, into an almost unbeatable force.

The Intel engineers, however, were not impressed. After a visit to the often chaotic Redmond headquarters, the Intel managers, who were used to the extreme neatness imposed by Andrew Grove, decided that the Washington company was a losing proposition. They strongly recommended that Intel turn down the offer. "My advice is an unqualified no," one of the engineers who visited Microsoft wrote in his report. "These people are flakes. They're not original, they don't really understand what they're doing, their ambitions are very low, and it's not really clear that they have succeeded even at that." After this report, Gates could not even get Andrew Grove to return his phone calls. This was the ominous beginning to a relationship that would grow even more tumultuous in the future.

Chapter Eight

Lost Memory

The arrangement to supply IBM with microprocessors was the beginning of a dramatic change in Intel's business. In 1980 they had been one of several suppliers of memory chips. Now the stage was set for them to become the world's pacesetter in new processor design. But this change took time, and was sometimes painful. As the decade of the 1980s continued, Intel's primary focus was still on the product it had first brought to market—memory chips.

But, as the processor market matured, demand for memory chips continued to drop, along with prices, in the face of the continuing over supply from Japan. Profits were shrinking, but Andrew didn't want to lay off employees. Instead, he requested that each worker contribute an extra two hours of work each day—without pay. Although Grove saw it as a way to protect jobs, or least said so publicly, some of the engineers complained that measures such as this made Intel an unpleasant place to work. A few protested the measure vocally but Andrew didn't care. He had always worked long hours himself, and saw no reason why everyone should not have to sacrifice during a business slowdown.

The slump in business turned out to be shortlived. As usual, the introduction of a new product made a big difference. Technological advance again spurted business growth; Moore's Law was still in full force. In March of 1983, Intel introduced a new processor in what they were calling the x86 line. The 80286 carried approximately 125,000 transistors and could address four billion bits of information. IBM quickly launched a new machine built around the 80286 and called it the PC AT (AT stood for Advanced Technology.) And most critically, the 80286 ran all the software written for the 8086 and 8088 processors.

When the 80286 was launched, Intel was selling over a billion dollars worth of chips a year. Twenty-one thousand people worked for the company. It was a highly competitive business that depended on its knowledge, or "intellectual property," to survive. Grove oversaw the creation of a large security operation that was aggressive in tracking down people who tried to sell stolen chips or, most dangerously, trade secrets to competitors. One of the security detail's tactics was to run "sting" operations, where they posed as buyers of the stolen merchandise in order to nab the thieves and spies. This level of security was an ominous sign to some veterans of the industry.

Also in 1983, Andrew published a book called *High-Output Management,* in which he summarized the lessons he had learned in the fifteen years he had been running Intel. As a way to explain his management methods he used simple examples, such as the difficulty of cooking a breakfast consisting of a three-minute soft-boiled egg, buttered toast and coffee so that all items were done at the same time and tasted good. This problem was similar, he said, to the effort it took to use employees, equipment and supplies to produce the best goods at the highest quantities at the least cost. In practice, he wrote, this meant concentrating on a daily flow of statistics rather than on soothing the feelings of his workers. In 1984, *FORTUNE Magazine* named him one of America's toughest bosses.

As the company was launching the 80286, Andrew was attempting once again to change a practice that had long bothered him. He tried to convince Noyce and Moore that it was time to end "second-sourcing" that forced Intel to license its products to another company. Andrew felt that they should be able to produce its own products and avoid relying on others to back them up. He did not like giving a competitor Intel's basic secrets.

But Noyce and Moore overruled him, as they had before. They argued that Intel still needed the money from licensing. They were also worried that customers might hesitate to buy their chips if there was any question about the reliability of the supply. It wouldn't be until 1985, when the 80386 chip went into production, that Andrew would finally be able to do away with second-sourcing.

In 1984, several Japanese firms were being accused before a congressional committee in Washington, by Bob Noyce and others, of dumping chips onto the American market. They also charged that this flooding of the market with memory chips sold at prices below cost was subsidized by the Japanese government. Representatives of the Japanese companies argued that the problem was that there were simply too many people in the world making chips.

No matter whose argument was believed, the memory chip business was no longer profitable. It became obvious that it was time for Intel to make a decision about the future of the company. Their allegiance to the memory chip was deep. It was the product that had launched the company. There was a historical, and even sentimental, attachment. Also, Grove was angry at what he considered to be the unfair trade practices of the Japanese.

But, by mid-1985, it became clear that it was time for Intel to change its business plan. The final decision came in a meeting that Grove remembered several years later. He and Gordon Moore were discussing the situation when Grove suddenly asked: "If I got kicked out and the board brought in a new CEO, what do you think he would do?" Moore answered quickly, "Get us out of memories [memory chips]."

After a moment Grove said: "Why shouldn't you and I walk out the door, come back and do it ourselves?"

At that point Intel was out of the memory chip business entirely. Now they could concentrate on their high-priced, high-profit line of microprocessor chips.

Concentrating on microprocessors did not eliminate all the competition, however. In 1984, Apple Computer launched the

Macintosh computer. The Mac revolutionized the desktop computer. Instead of a green or amber screen that waited for the user to type a string of letters and numbers separated by back slashes, the Mac booted up to a blue screen dotted with easy to use icons that you clicked on with a mouse. Words typed onto a Mac appeared exactly as they did on paper, an idea that came to be called WYSIWYG (What You See Is What You Get). The Mac was simply much more easy and fun to use than the IBM PC and the dozens of so-called IBM clones that had popped onto the market since 1981. And, most ominously, the Mac used a Motorola processor.

The Mac accounted for only one in seven computers sold. But Intel knew that the usability advantages of the Mac threatened the future of the Intel based computers. They also knew that it would be months, if not years, before someone created a similar program to run on the PC. For the first time, Intel was realizing that its future was dependent on many factors beyond its control, such as software design and the price of computers.

The mid-1980s were a difficult period. At the 1986 shareholder meeting, Grove said, "We're pleased to report 1986 is over. It was, without question, the toughest year in Intel's history, filled with plant closings, layoffs and deep losses." The loss of the memory chip business had led to severe cut-backs. The company wisely never stopped investing in research and development, however.

Other problems popped up during these years. When the next generation of processor, the 80386, was released, IBM resisted

In 1984 Steve Jobs announced the release of the Macintosh Computer. Based on a Motorola processor, Grove saw the "Mac" as a direct threat to the future of Intel.

putting it into their new microcomputers. They feared that such a powerful desktop machine—the 386 was a thirty-two bit processor that could use more than one operating system simultaneously—would hurt sales of their larger computers, which sold for thousands more than did the PC.

This decision lost IBM its dominant position in the microcomputer market. When Compaq, who had simply built cheaper versions of what IBM had already produced at this point, began using the 386 in their desktop machines, "Big Blue" was left behind. Suddenly, Intel was no longer under IBM's shadow. Other computer manufacturers began ordering the 386 in even greater quantities than IBM. Now Intel and Microsoft were the two companies blazing the trail for the fast growing small computer industry.

At the same time, the strains in the relationship between Intel and Microsoft continued. Although Intel engineers still had little respect for Microsoft's software, the DOS operating system had become the industry standard for PCs. Microsoft had grown into the dominant software company in the world. It's highly aggressive chairman, Bill Gates, thought that every dollar that Intel extracted from a buyer for a new chip would be one less dollar that could be spent for Microsoft software. He wanted Intel to slow the development of new processors, and to sell more of the less expensive chips. From Intel's point of view, the push for development was critical. If they did not develop new products, Motorola or another competitor would. The high prices they charged for their newest chips paid for the intensive research and development, as well as the construction of the giant fabrication plants that usually cost two billion dollars to build. This all depended on maintaining a high demand for new chips.

Microsoft had different priorities than Intel because they were not only creating new programs, they were also supplying software to users of computers based on older, less powerful processors, such as the 8086 and the 286. Intel was afraid that software companies would make their programs work more efficiently with the old chips. This would lessen demand for their new products, which were the most profitable.

There were efforts to keep the peace between the two companies. This was difficult because both Grove and Gates had volatile tempers. When their aides arranged meetings to talk and to reduce the tensions, the situation often grew worse. On one occasion, when Grove invited Gates to his house for lunch in the mid-1980s, the conversation became so heated that the food was barely touched. At one point, the caterers hurried into the dining room to find out what all the shouting was about.

While Gates and Grove may not have liked it, Intel and Microsoft were locked together. No one else had their influence on the computer industry. As they moved into the future, Grove and Gates eyed one another warily, like boxers in a ring, as each worked to push technology into new, unexpected directions.

Chapter Nine

Groving

1986 was a tough year for Intel. The financial losses due to the loss of the memory chip business, the continuing conflict with Microsoft, and the huge effort necessary to stay atop the furious pace of technological development, had exhausted Grove. He seriously considered retiring. But by the next year, he decided the challenge of building Intel was too powerful to resist. He knew it was not yet time to quit. When the company officially recognized his nearly twenty years of successful management on May 21, 1987, he was named chief executive officer. Once again, his real status—he had been running the company for many years—was simply being acknowledged.

By this time, Grove had returned the company to profitability. With the company's numbers back in the black, he also relaxed some of the restrictions he had imposed on employees. One concession was the building of showers on the company's campus for those who liked to exercise before or after work or on their breaks. Before, he had worried that this would distract people from their work.

Another reason he stayed was that much remained to be done. For example, while the 386 chips were selling rapidly, manufacturing efficiency, as measured by percentage of wafers of silicon that had to be thrown away, was still considerably below that of the Japanese. This problem especially irked Grove.

One nagging practice that Grove was finally able to end was second-sourcing. Because Intel owned the copyrights, keeping competitors out of the market allowed Intel to charge what the market would bear for its processors. They could sell the 386 for $900, even though it cost them only $141 to make. In contrast, versions of the old 8086 chip were selling for only $4.06. In order to maintain control of the chip "architecture," Intel's lawyers were constantly in court suing competitors for patent or licensing violations.

Grove wanted to speed up the shift from the 286 to the 386.The profit margins were much higher on the new chip. He encouraged all PC manufacturers to start selling more 386 machines. But several manufacturers complained that they were still doing well with the 286 based computers and saw no reason to spend the money necessary to promote the more powerful processors.

Grove then tried a new strategy, one that altered the way Intel did business. Instead of working exclusively with the computer makers, he decided to advertise the newer processor directly to the consumer. The idea was that the consumer would then ask for the new, more powerful chip. This would pressure the computer companies to order the 386 from Intel.

Several thought this was an idea that was sure to fail. Never before had a "high technology" company attempted to market its products directly to the end user. The typical strategy was to sell to the limited number of manufacturers. The cost of this type of marketing was relatively inexpensive. Now Andy Grove wanted to spend millions to advertise on television? What did the average person know about computer hardware? To most of the industry, and the computer press, this seemed like a gigantic waste of money.

They were wrong. The new marketing strategy worked beyond anyone's wildest dreams. Consumers, both personal and business, were eager to buy, but were still uncertain about the new technology. The idea of buying a brand name appealed to the average consumer, and after the demise of IBM many shoppers did not recognize the prevalent computer names. The advertising campaign convinced them that buying a machine with a 386 Intel microprocessor was safe. Soon, most of the computer manufacturers were clamoring to have the little Intel sticker on their products.

Later, Grove began a new advertising campaign based around the slogan "Intel Inside." Within a year, surveys revealed that the word Intel and the slogan "Intel Inside" ranked as the third most recognizable brand name in the country. Even most computer makers, who had originally been angered by Intel's attempt to force them to build different computers, came to realize that it was to their advantage to have customers demanding new chips. This usually meant more sales, as users rushed

Microsoft's release of the Windows system for the PC increased the demand for more powerful processors.

to have the latest, most powerful processor in their computers.

In 1989, Intel brought out the 486, which would prove to be the last of the numbered chips. From this point on the chips would be named, which were far easier to copyright. Grove learned this lesson when a judge ruled that the "x86" designation was so commonly used that Intel had lost the exclusive right to use it on their chips.

Now Andrew knew that Intel itself would have to create the demand for new, more powerful chips. In 1991, he created the Intel Architecture Labs to research and develop a variety of products that would increase the market for Intel chips. One project involved the delivery of video from the Internet, "streaming media," that does not have to finish downloading onto a computer's hard disk before it can be played. Another product made it easier to make long-distance phone calls on the Internet by standardizing the programs used to connect the calls. A third made it easier to use a "videophone" on the Internet, so you can see the person you're talking to.

That same year, Andrew showed a gathering of computer industry people how a notebook PC equipped with special chips could receive E-mail messages and graphics delivered over a wireless network from satellites or ground transmitters.

By the early 1990s, Intel's control of the pace of computer hardware development was unchallenged. Never before had a company that made a product most people would never understand had such a recognizable name and exalted position in the world economy.

In the process of building Intel, Andrew had become immensely wealthy, with a fortune of $300 million. He wasn't the only Intel employee to prosper, because of the company's stock option plan, there are thousands of Intel millionaires.

Money, and the things it buys, has never been important to Andrew, however. He lives in an ordinary house, not a mansion, and he doesn't buy private planes or sports cars. He and his wife, Eva, plan to leave most of their money to charity. Already they have remembered the organizations that helped them in their early years. They funded chemistry scholarships at the City College of New York and have made generous contributions to the International Rescue Committee, which brought Andrew from Vienna to America.

Andrew's life at work was modest, too. His office was the standard eight foot by nine foot Intel cubicle. If he arrived at work late, he looked for a space just like everyone else. There are no assigned parking places at Intel. He usually stayed late at work, frequently until after eight p.m. He also taught a popular management course at nearby Stanford University.

When he wasn't working in his cubicle or teaching, the 5' 9" Andrew skied, biked with Eva, read thrillers, worked out, and listened to opera or pop music soundtracks from the 1960s. He also likes to dance. His two daughters call his disjointed dance step "Groving" instead of grooving. "He was a wonderful father," his older daughter remembers. Says his younger,"Being Andrew Grove's child isn't for the faint of heart. But if you can roll with it, it's great." When he traveled out of the country on business, he always tried to include the kids. He made the girls write reports on the countries they visited and to encourage them, he paid a nickel a page. "That's how we'd get our spending money," they remember.

One of Grove's daughter remembers that at her wedding reception her father grabbed a silver-lame cape and rhinestone tiara and took to the center of the dance floor where he "Groved" to a disco song. His children also remember him as a comfortable, relaxed man whose face was usually wrinkled into a smile.

Chapter Ten

Division

In 1993 Intel released the first of its named processors. The Pentium used three million transistors to process 100 million instructions per second. It was twenty times as fast as the 286. Although some thought the Pentium to be a disappointment, the "Intel Inside" campaign and the huge installed base of computers already using Intel's earlier chips, almost guaranteed that it would be successful.

The product was released with a huge promotional campaign and was an immediate success. All seemed to be going well. The last thing Grove expected was a public-relations disaster.

The trouble started in November of 1994 when a professor of mathematics, who had been using the new chip for high-level calculations, discovered that it could make a mathematical error when it was doing elaborate long-division problems. His first reaction was to call the Intel help line, where his complaint was ignored. Next, he posted his findings on the Internet. Soon the company was getting calls from Pentium users concerned about the problem.

Intel management and engineers had known about the problem before the professor called. It resulted from an error in the math floating point unit, a section of the Pentium that contained a "lookup table" of solutions to mathematical equations. But they assumed that the chances of the flaw resulting in the wrong solution was so rare—one occurrence every nine billion calculations by their internal estimates—that they decided to not scrap the millions of flawed chips. The average Pentium owner should encounter a problem only once every twenty-seven thousand years. The vast majority of PCs containing the flawed Pentium chips would be scrapped before even a fraction noticed the error.

But there were users who needed precision: Graphic designers, typographers, engineers, economists, financial analysts, rocket designers and scientists would find errors more common and far more serious. Intel planned to replace these faulty processors when the users could prove that they did high-level calculations on their machines.

This attitude infuriated many users, especially the more technically savvy ones who complained on the web pages set up to discuss Intel. Eventually, these users began notifying the large media outlets, such as CNN and *The New York Times.*

Soon the Internet was filled with Intel jokes. For example:
Q. Have you heard about Intel's new salary plan for its workers?
A. You can pick up your paycheck every other Friday, but only if you can prove you really NEED it.
Q. Why didn't Intel call the Pentium the 586?

A. Because they added 486 and 100 on the first Pentium and got 585.99999.

Q. What does Pentium stand for?

A. Perfect Enough for Nine out of Ten Instructors at the University of Montana, or: Practically Everyone Now Thinks It's Useless for Math.

Grove was on a Christmas ski trip when the story broke into the wider media outlets. CNN reporters showed up at the company headquarters, seeking a corporate response to a negative story they had already prepared. Grove and other Intel management began working to describe the nature of the problem and why their solution was the most practical for everyone. After a few days of news stories, the furor began to die down.

Then IBM announced that they would not ship anymore computers with the Pentium processor until Intel developed what they considered a better response to the controversy. In other words, replace the faulty chips or else. Many observers thought that IBM, who was still angry over the way Intel had marketed the 386 chip years before, had seized the chance to hit Intel when they were vulnerable. Any damage to the Intel brand name may benefit other easily recognizable names in the computer industry, such as IBM.

Grove met with his top managers and decided to change the way they had dealt with the crisis. Intel announced that they would replace all of the flawed Pentiums, no questions asked. IBM had forced them to "bite the bullet." To avoid the chances of more bad news, the company even offered to come to people's home and change the chips. The decision to replace the Pentiums was expected to cost $475 million. Grove said later that the entire experience was "a difficult education."

It is ironic to note that the entire episode may have rebounded to Intel's benefit. The company name became better known than ever, and once they agreed to replace the chips, customers felt like it was a company that would go to great lengths to correct their problems.

The Pentium fiasco proved that the conflict and competition in the processor market was just as, if not more, fierce than it had been in the memory chip business. In 1995 a new threat appeared on the horizon. Many critics and analysts thought that the RISC (Reduced Instruction Set Computing) processor, developed by Motorola, was far superior. When IBM, Motorola and Apple had formed an alliance to produce the PowerPC 601 using the RISC processor, Grove called the Intel managers into a long meeting.

Motorola claimed the RISC offered Pentium-class performance at half of the cost. Motorola had proven expertise in chip fabrication because of the Mac. IBM certainly had the ability to market a computer, and although Apple had made several bad marketing decisions, most still thought it was the most innovative computer company in the world. The PowerPC 601 presented a taunting threat to the hegemony of the Pentium. This was the problem Grove presented to his managers.

Instead of retreating in the face of the competition, they decided to dramatically increase Intel's advertising budget.

Andrew Grove in 1996.

Grove gave interviews to the computer press and used other means to convince his customers that changing processors would result in them losing sales. Too many people trusted the Intel name—and there was always the problem of compatibility to consider.

What finally removed the threat of the PowerPC was the failure of Motorola to build a promised follow-up chip, the 604, that offered more than a 15% performance improvement over Pentium chips. The threat from the PowerPC had stayed around long enough to convince Grove to bring back some of his old rules at Intel. He wanted to refocus people on "the basics." There were also changes made to the processor. Chip size shrank, increasing both speed—because electrons had to travel a shorter distance—and the number of chips that could be made from a single wafer.

The cost of the Pentium was cut repeatedly, especially after the release of yet a new processor with 5 million transistors. The Pentium "Pro" was for the most sophisticated computers, such as the ones used by engineers and high level graphic artists. The "Pro" was considerably faster than the Motorola RISC chips that had threatened Intel's market. Once again, there was no reason for most computer manufacturers to look elsewhere for their chips. Intel had risen to another challenge.

As the threat from the RISC processor disappeared, Grove again focused on the need to increase the size of the overall chip market. The architecture lab Andrew had started in 1991 produced few products that immediately made money for Intel. But it was encouraging the computer industry to create exciting new hardware and software products that would entice users into upgrading their systems—thus increasing business for everyone.

There was also a lessening of the tensions between Intel and Microsoft. To avoid incidents like that meal-time shouting match of a decade earlier, the two companies arranged regular meetings between the Grove and Gates' assistants. This way topics to be discussed between the two CEOs could be settled before they met. This tightened agenda helped keep the meetings out of areas that could erupt into anger.

Gates and Grove began meeting two or three times a year. There was much to talk about—their interests still did not totally coincide. Intel's profits still depended on selling newer and more powerful chips. But Microsoft could, as always, make money by continuing to provide programming for the 250 million machines already using older processors.This was the biggest point of contention between the companies.

After a series of meetings, Microsoft and Intel finally started to agree on ways to stimulate demand for PCs. They failed to arrive at any settlement about what they saw as the future of the Internet, however. Microsoft wants to control the browser market—the software that provides entry to the Internet. Intel is focused simply on technical innovation, and would prefer that no single software company dominate in browsers. This should insure that the market will grow faster, increasing the demand for even more hardware advancements. This is the type of question the two companies will continue to argue about into the twentieth-first century.

In 1996, Grove learned that he had prostate cancer. It was not immediately life-threatening, and the doctors offered a variety of ways to fight the disease. Never one to sit idly by, Grove decided to learn everything he could about the disease. He went to the library and, as he remarked later: "I read until I found that when I picked up an article, I had read it. I hadn't done that much research since I got my Ph.D." He and Eva visited the library at Stanford University weekly to read the latest research findings. He wound up treating the cancer with a new high-dose radiation therapy.

The cancer forced him to reappraise his lifestyle. He now eats a low fat diet with lots of tofu, vegetables and fruit. He also takes antioxidant pills. Always active, he stays trim bicycling, skiing, jogging, kayaking and swimming.

In the spring of 1997, he found a research study that linked calcium intake to the spread of prostate cancer through the rest of the body. After he became convinced that the study was valid, he persuaded several physicians specializing in prostate cancer to reverse their recommendation to take calcium. He takes a blood test for the cancer every four months. "When I enter the month of the test, my stress notches up. And then as I get closer, I get more nervous. And then when they draw the blood, it's unimaginable—a new level of anxiety starts, and it continues until I get my results back," he said in a recent interview.

Chapter Eleven

Retirement

In November 1996 Andrew Grove made a multimedia presentation at Comdex, the computer industry's leading trade show. The subject of the presentation was how far Intel and the industry had come in twenty-five years. Grove, now sixty, looked very little like the young man with the thick glasses, gold chains and bushy hairstyle who had joined Intel in 1968. He was well groomed, tanned and lean. Even the heavy accent of his youth had largely disappeared.

Grove had also become a public figure. His photo showed up often on the covers of business magazines. He was adored by the Intel shareholders—their shares had increased 40% each year over the last decade. He was the undisputed leader of the company. It filled him with pride to be recognized as the guiding genius of Intel's success.

Intel was the most profitable company in the computer industry. There were now thousands of Intel millionaires.

In May of 1997 Andrew became chairman as well as CEO. He hand picked his heir-apparent, Craig Barrett, to become company president. This change was a clear signal that the day was approaching when he would retire and devote himself to other interests. But he still ran the company with a strong, steady hand. One writer described his performance at Board of Director meetings to be like "a mixture of showmanship and brainpower, as if Albert Einstein were guest host of the Tonight Show."

The challenges are never-ending. As Andrew moved up to chairman in May 1998, inexpensive PCs that relied on low-end chips were becoming popular. This threatened the company's profit margins.

To meet this challenge Intel quickly unveiled its first new microprocessor in five years. The Celeron was cheaper than the Pentium and it lacked the on-board memory designed to handle three-dimensional graphics and video. It was designed for the less expensive computers whose users did not need the power of a Pentium.

The Celeron was a simplified Pentium Pro. By giving it another name, Intel hoped to avoid cutting into sales of its top processor. The name Celeron, it was hoped, would suggest both "acceleration" and "cell"—exciting, scientific-sounding names.

Another challenge facing Intel is the transition to network computing. Intel had been slow to respond to the changes that will be created by having dozens of keyboards and monitors connected to a central computer.

A more ominous threat on the horizon is a new federal government investigation to determine if Intel is monopolizing the microprocessor market. This was not the first time the question of Intel's monopoly power has been investigated.

Previous investigations had come to nothing. Now the government is questioning Intel's relationship with Microsoft, whose Windows graphical interface is used on more than 90% of the world's computers. Critics of the two powerhouses refer to the combination as "Wintel," and have complained often and loudly about what they consider to be unfair competitive practices. The investigators from the U.S. Justice Department charged with enforcing the anti-trust laws that seek to keep a few companies from controlling an entire industry were looking to see if the two were dividing the computer market between them.

Grove had been able to divert such investigations in the past. His chief strategy had been to keep everything secret. Managers were warned to watch what they said, because a competitor might be listening. He even went so far as to stage mock investigations and trials. Intel staff played the role of law enforcement officials entering an executive's office to seal it off and to take away documents. These scenarios emphasized the point that Intel was under pressure to protect itself.

Another continuous pressure was to continue innovating. New applications for microchips is critical to the company's future.They employ one thousand chip designers, and spend about two billion dollars a year on research and development.

One result of the devotion to new product development was the Pentium II, released in 1996. It boasted seven million transistors and can make 588 million calculations a second. The next year, Intel demonstrated a seven hundred megahertz chip that with the calculating power of some of the most expensive chips and can easily handle voice-recognition programs.

Also in the design stages is the new Merced chip that, for the first time since the 8086, makes basic changes in the x86 architecture. Production of the Merced will end Intel's strategy of backward-compatibility, and the computer manufacturers have been slow to encourage its development. Whether a new company will respond to the Merced as Compaq did with the 386 over a decade ago has yet to be determined.

Andrew predicts that the Intel chip of the year 2011 will have one billion transistors (compared to the current 5.5 million) and will reach a speed of 10,000 megahertz.

The company is also working closely with Hollywood. Its Media Lab will help movie makers come up with new ideas and images for special effects movies. The long-term goal, though, is to create a sophisticated multimedia computer that can do far more with graphics and interactivity than any existing system. It will be powered by an advanced version of the new MMX (for multimedia extension) technology, Intel's multimedia-enhanced microprocessor line that is designed to make music sound more resonant, video images flow more smoothly and graphics colors look richer.

Intel continues to invest heavily in small companies that design interactive programming for the Internet, including live broadcasts of concerts and dramas on the Web. The company is working with Disney to design new ways of distributing the studio's programs electronically. It is designing an electronic videoconferencing network for the World Economic Forum, an

Criag Barrett replaced Grove as CEO of Intel in 1998.

influential group of CEOs and government leaders. It has also helped Starbucks, the nationwide chain of coffee stores, to build a network that would link together selected cafes and allow coffee lovers to send and receive video E-mail.

Intel has a seventy person software lab in Shanghai developing multimedia and 3-D content in Chinese. Andrew envisions a future in which we watch TV on our PCs, play games on the Internet, use computers to manage appliances, and talk with friends and family using Internet videophones. Clearly, the company has gone beyond its origins as a chip company.

Intel also works closely with the elementary and high schools in the areas where it has plants. In order to produce the workers and consumers the company will need in the future, it has been providing resources-equipment, training and teachers, to build interest in math, science and technology. High school students are invited to work in Intel plants as interns, and high school science teachers can work in the plants during the summer.

By helping to train the students, Intel can contribute both to its own growth and profitability and to the growth of the American economy as communications technology play an ever-larger role in our daily lives. High-technology companies, like phone and computer companies, have been contributing 30% of America's economic growth in recent years. It's one of the few areas of the economy where products tend to cost less year after year. This helps the United States stay a leader in the world economy, and it helps reduce inflation.

The powerful role that Intel plays in the world economy, and the prestige that its leader has earned as the vision of his company's amazing growth, motivated *Time* magazine to name Andrew Grove as its 1997 Man of the Year. This prestigious acknowledgement of his influence—other selections have been Ted Turner, Pope John II, and Jimmy Carter—made the Intel president a much more recognizable public character. *Time* cited his vision and determination, and his influence on the future of a new world economy, as its reasons for making the choice.

Andrew surprised many when he gave up the job of CEO in May 1998, but he retained the title of chairman. For the first time in thirty years, he won't be running the company on a day-to-day basis. That won't keep him from constantly focusing Intel's attention on the long-range picture. To others in the computer industry who worry about the company's market power he says only, "We have a very crass reason to be a driving force. We build large factories and we have to fill them. It can't scare you when you don't have a choice."

As for the future, he says, "I have a rule in my business: to see what can happen in the next ten years, look at what has happened in the last ten years." In the past ten years, he turned a growing company into a global dynamo that is leading the United States and the world into the Age of Information. Intel's challenge is to continue this phenomenal growth into the next century without the strong leadership of Andrew Grove.

Computer Industry Timeline

1946—ENIAC, the first general purpose electronic computer, is used to generate ballistics information. Using vacuum tubes to store data, it can run to 300 multiplications per second, but takes up a whole room and gave out more heat than a home sauna.

1947—The transistor—crucial for computers because it allows miniaturization and controls current flow in electronic equipment—is invented.

1957—Responding to the Soviet Union's Sputnik launch, U.S. forms Advanced Research Projects Agency (ARPA) in Department of Defense to bolster science and technology applicable to military.

1958—First integrated circuit—device crucial to today's computing revolution—is demonstrated.

1968—Intel, the Silicon Valley company that would come to dominate the semiconductor industry, is founded.

1969—Defense Department contracts business, academic and government researchers to collaborate on ARPANET, forerunner of today's Internet. Researchers at four campuses create ARPANET's first "host" computers, connecting Stanford Research Institute, UCLA, UC-Santa Barbara and the University of Utah.

1971—Intel markets the 4004, the first microprocessor or "computer on a chip." It has 23,000 transistors and is used in early calculators. One chip has twice the processing power of ENIAC and is one thousandth its size.

1972—IBM introduces floppy disks. Public demonstration of ARPANET in Washington, D.C. First e-mail message sent via ARPANET

1974—Intel 8080 uses 60,000 transistors. It will be used in the first kit computers.

1975—The first do-it-yourself personal computer, the Altair 8800, is introduced. Microsoft is founded.

1977—Three preassembled personal computers is introduced: Commodore's PET, Apple Computer's Apple II and Radio Shack's TRS 80.

1978—Intel introduces 8086 microprocessor, first of popular "x86" chips that will power most of the world's personal computers. Apple introduces the floppy disk drive.

1979—VisiCalc, the first spreadsheet program for personal computers, is marketed. Usenet, a system for computer bulletin boards called newsgroups, is established.

1980—Seagate Technology offers the first low-cost hard disk. ARPANET spans the country, connecting more than 400 host computers at university, government and military sites. More than 10,000 people have access.

1981—On August 12, IBM introduces the PC, which uses the Intel 8088 Modems for personal computers introduced.

1982—Compaq brings out the first IBM clone. Transmission Control Protocol and Internet Protocol, the system commonly known today as TCP/IP and which computer networks use to communicate with one another on the Internet is established for ARPANET.

1983—Apple introduces the Lisa, bringing the mouse to personal computers. (At $10,000, Lisa was a failure.) IBM markets the PC-AT, the first personal computer with a built-in hard disk.

1984—Apple introduces the Macintosh, making Lisa technology affordable. Hewlett-Packard Co. sells the first low-cost laser printer, the LaserJet. Intel 80286 has 134,000 transistors. National Science Foundation creates NSFNET, which links five university supercomputer centers and connects with ARPANET. William Gibson coins the term "cyberspace" in his novel _Neuromancer_. Apple introduces the Macintosh personal computer.

1985—Intel rolls out its 80386 microprocessor, which facilitated the first truly speedy personal computers. Microsoft Windows 1.0 is released.

1987—Apple's new Macintosh II and Macintosh SE computers become the most powerful personal computers available. Number of Internet host computers tops 10,000.

1989—Apple introduces the Macintosh Portable. First relays between commercial e-mail carriers (MCI and Compuserve) and the Internet.

1990—IBM and Apple market inexpensive personal computers, the PS/1 and the Macintosh Classic. Intel's new 80486 has 1,200,000 transistors. The World, first commercial provider of Internet dial-up access, goes online. Archie, a system for finding files on the Internet, is released.

1991—World Wide Web files are made available on the Internet. National Science Foundation lifts restrictions on commercial use of NSFNET, a major step toward commercialization of the Internet. Gopher, a popular menu system for finding information on the Internet, is introduced.

1992—Internet Society, dedicated to growth and evolution of the Internet, is chartered. Number of host computers breaks 1 million.

1993—Intel Pentium has 3,300,000 transistors. InterNIC, repository of information about the Internet and the place where Internet names are registered, is created. The White House comes online at http://www.whitehouse.gov/. More than 100 countries are now connected to the Internet. Mosaic, a program for reading information on the Internet, is introduced.

1994—ARPANET/Internet celebrates 25th anniversary. Commercial Internet users now outnumber research and academic users by 2-1.

1995—National Science Foundation steps out of Internet "backbone" business as traffic shifts to commercial providers.

1996—Intel Pentium Pro has 5,500,000 transistors.

Glossary

Binary number system: A system using only two digits (0 and 1) to represent all numbers. Used in computers because an electrical circuit has two states—on and off.

Bit: The smallest unit of information in a computer. It's an abbreviation for Binary digIT.

Byte: A string of bits, usually eight, that represents a number or character.

Central processing unit: The part of a computer that executes instructions.

Chip: An electronic circuit on a tiny piece of semiconductor material, usually silicon.

Clone: A computer that can run the same software as IBM's personal computers.

DRAM: Dynamic Random Access Memory—a memory chip invented by Intel used by programs during calculations.

EPROM: Erasable Programmable Read-Only Memory—storage memory invented by Intel

Floppy disk: A flexible disk covered in cardboard or plastic. It is used to store data or instructions. Most programs are sold on floppy disks.

Hard disk: A sealed disk used to store data or instructions. It costs more than a floppy disk but stores more information and works faster.

Hardware: The physical parts of a computer system, such as the keyboard.

Keyboard: Typewriter-like device for putting data into a computer or giving it commands.

Kilobyte: 1,024 bytes.

Laser printer: A printer that uses a laser to print.

Megabyte: One million bytes.

Memory: The part of the computer where data or instructions are stored in binary form.

Microprocessor: A single chip that has all the functions of a computer's central processing unit.

MIPS: "million instructions per second," a measure of chip speed.

Modem: A device that moves information between computers, usually over telephone lines.

Monitor: A television-like screen that displays data.

Mouse: A hand-held device that moves the cursor on a computer screen.

Operating system: A program that controls all other programs run on a computer screen.

Peripherals: External devices used with a computer, such as monitors and modems.

Personal computer: A desktop or portable computer intended for use by an individual.

Printer: A device that prints numbers, letters or graphic images from a computer.

Program: Instructions that tell a computer how to do something. For example: a word processing program tells a computer how to work with text.

ROM: Read Only Memory. Permanent data or instructions that users can't alter.

RAM: Random Access Memory. Temporary memory that users can retrieve and alter.

Software: Computer programs.

Bibliography

"Andrew Grove: All Computing Will Take Place In a Connected Setting that Places New Requirements On Everything," David S. Jackson, *Global Business Report/ Movers and Shakers*, March 3, 1997

"Andrew Grove: Man of the Year," Walter Isaacson, Norman Pearlstine and Joshua Cooper Ramo, *Time*, December 29, 1997.

"Behind the Wave: Consequences of the Digital Age," by Christopher H. Schmitt et. al., *The San Jose Mercury News*, March 2, 1997.

"Birth of the Super Chip," Mike Bracken, *Focus* (London), September, 1996.

"Chip Off The Old Block?," Michael Krantz, *Time*, May 26, 1997.

"Davos Agenda '97: I.T. At The Top" Andrew Grove, et. al., *World Link*, January/February 1997.

"Electronic School," Karen Southwick, *The American School Board Journal*, March 1997.

"The Future of the PC," Brenton R. Schlender, *Fortune*, Aug. 26, 1991.

"Have You Used Your 4 Million Transistors Yet This Year?," *Engineering & Science*, Fall 1988.

Inside Intel, Jackson, Tim. Dutton: New York, New York, 1997.

"Intel's Amazing Profit Machine," David Kirkpatrick, *Fortune*, February 17, 1997.

Only The Paranoid Survive, Grove, Andrew S. New York: Doubleday, 1996.

"Personal Computers," Rory J. O'Connor, The San Jose Mercury News, Aug. 11, 1991.

Index

DATE DUE			